Armen and L⟨ Guide

Table of Contents

4

Aloha!

 We're Armen and Lori Stein. We've visited Kauai many times over the years, including living there for 2½ months in 2011. We think we bring a balanced perspective to visiting the Garden Isle. We're from the mainland (Seattle), so we look at things from a visitor's point of view. But we've lived on and visited Kauai enough to get a real sense of the island and to try many different things – some of them multiple times!

We love talking to people about Kauai. In this guide we'll imagine that you are planning a trip to Kauai, and you came over for a glass of wine or a cup of coffee to talk about it.

The other guidebooks try to be complete references – they try to include **everything**. We don't. This book is a shorter list of our very favorite places to see and things to do. But even with the shorter list, don't try to do it all in one visit! Kauai is a place to relax, unwind and enjoy the spirit of aloha. You'll come back.

Stay in touch on our Facebook page! It's the same name as this book. Let us know about your visit to Kauai, or if you agree or disagree with what we've said. Things can change on Kauai between updates to this guide, and we want you to have the latest info. We'll post photos and updates there, and answer any questions we can.

> Tip: If you're reading this as an ebook and you want to see a higher-resolution version of a photo, click on it. If your device supports it and you have an internet

connection, you'll see the same photo on our Facebook page.

Why Kauai?

We didn't choose Kauai – it chose us. The first time we visited in 1994, it was a gift of a timeshare week from Armen's parents. It was a short-notice booking, and we specified that we would take *any condo* on *any island* in Hawaii. We figured that we would end up on Oahu, Maui or the Big Island – those were really the only islands we were familiar with. We were puzzled when a condo came up in a place called Poipu Beach on an island named Kauai. We actually had to look up Kauai to learn about it.

When we arrived, Kauai was still recovering from Hurricane Iniki that hit the island hard in 1992. (The storm scenes in Jurassic Park were filmed as Iniki approached – Spielberg decided to stay and shoot rather than evacuate.) Even though two years had passed, many roofs were still covered in blue tarps, and several hotels were eerily dark and deserted behind chain link fencing.

But the natural beauty and resilient spirit of Kauai was undeniable. Since then we've visited the Big Island and Honolulu, but we've still never made it to Maui. Nothing against Maui – we just choose to spend our limited time and money going back to Kauai.

Is Kauai For You?

When people ask us about whether we think they would like Kauai, we usually ask them a few questions before we answer. Do they like fancy restaurants, night clubs, music, and entertainment? Then they might find Kauai a little sleepy. As we like to say, "The island closes at 9." There isn't much in the way of night life after sunset. It's peaceful and quiet. When we visit, we adjust to getting up early with the sunrise, and getting to sleep by 10pm or so.

Kauai is naturally cooled by the trade breezes. There isn't much air conditioning in shops, houses and condos. There are plenty of walks, hikes, beaches and simple activities like kayaking, snorkeling, ziplining and bicycling. There's no parasailing or jet skiing on Kauai – they're banned, and we're fine with that.

If you like a relaxed and rural experience, where you can still find an uncrowded beach, a dirt road, a quiet park, and authentic people, then Kauai may be just your thing.

An Unofficial Companion

The only Kauai book you really need is The Ultimate Kauai Guidebook (UKG) by Andrew Doughty. It isn't perfect, but we think it's the best one. We recommend you buy the latest edition now and get familiar with it before you go, but if you don't, they sell it at the Kauai Costco. In this guide we'll refer to the UKG often.

We'll rarely give exact directions and addresses in this guide. We figure you'll use your smartphone or the UKG to find things.

Kauai Lessons

Kauai is a place to truly relax and unplug from your everyday mainland worries. If you're open to it, the beauty of the island and the friendly, independent spirit of its residents will help you to disconnect from the mainland and all of its concerns.

Money Stress

On one of our visits when our kids were young, we were stressed about our finances. We owned our own business (still do) and although we'd been doing fine when we had planned our vacation, now that we were on the island, things were tight. One morning we took the kids to Salt Pond Park to go swimming. Armen forgot that he had $15 in cash in his swimming trunks, and soon he discovered that the money was gone – obviously it was lost in the ocean.

Armen was pretty upset that he had been so careless and lost the money. We drove the 12 miles back to Poipu, and decided to get some lunch at the walk-up window at a Mexican place. As we were waiting to order, we struck up a conversation with a couple that got in line right behind us. They asked how our day was going, and still smarting from the loss of the cash, Armen mentioned it to them.

They said "Wait, was that at Salt Ponds? Was it $15? We were there too, and we found your money floating in the water!" And they gave the salty money back to us.

It's hard to describe the odds against this happening – the beach was miles away, nowhere near this tiny restaurant. The fact that we all ended up at the same place at exactly the same time is remarkable. Our lesson? That if we were going to fret about something like $15, the island was just going to give it back to us. Now what should we worry about?

Island Time

During another visit, Armen was focused on time. A lot. Maybe his brain was still on the mainland with all its schedules and punctuality. He was thinking about times for snorkeling, dinner, sunset – everything. When he came back from swimming in the ocean, he realized that his waterproof watch was gone. It had fallen off in the ocean. Take that, punctuality! Later when we were talking to a local woman, she said that Pele (the goddess of fire and volcanos, and the creator of the Hawaiian Islands) had taken the watch as an offering. Armen managed to have a great time for the rest of our visit without knowing what time it was.

Now when we arrive on Kauai, we are able to slip into Island Time before we walk out of the airport. You can do this too – we recommend that you practice by going to Kauai as often as you can.

All those Apostrophes

It seems just about every Hawaiian word has an apostrophe. Even the word Kaua'i has one. It just means a quick stop. For example, Ke'e Beach is pronounced "Kay AY" with a little stop between the two syllables. We'll leave the apostrophes out of most words in this guide unless we think they're helpful.

> Tip: Pee Road in Poipu is actually Pe'e Road, pronounced "Pay AY". Don't be juvenile.

Where to Stay

You may already have your place booked, but if not, we recommend staying in condos. A condo is often cheaper than a nice hotel, but you get a full kitchen, more room, more personality, and more freedom. They usually have community barbecues to grill your fish. For a good selection, check out the Parrish Collection. There are also houses and condos for rent on VRBO if you know where you want to stay.

In general, we like staying in the Poipu area on the south shore. It's generally sunnier and drier there, though it can rain at any time anywhere on Kauai. Some folks really like the lush north shore, around Princeville or Hanalei, or the convenience and central location of Kapa'a on the east shore. It's just a matter of preference – anyplace on Kauai is great.

We're partial to Waikomo Stream Villas for the price and the awesome walkable location at the Poipu round-about, but they don't have ocean views or fancy amenities, and there can be some road noise. We stay there and spend our savings on other things. The property is easy walking distance to three beaches (Sheraton, Baby and Lawai Road/Beach House), snorkeling at Koloa Landing, and grocery stores, shops, restaurants and bars at the round-about.

> Tip: If you're okay with stairs, an upstairs unit will have more privacy and fewer mosquitos than a ground-level unit.

A lot of people look for a place that has air conditioning. It's really not necessary on Kauai, and many places don't have it. Air conditioners remove some of the essence of Kauai. It rarely gets very hot anyway, and the trade winds keep the air breezy most of the time. If the room has a ceiling fan, as most do, you'll be fine. We find that we adapt after a day or two.

Kauai Wildlife

No, we're not talking about night clubs and dance parties – Kauai doesn't really have many of those. We're referring to animals.

Kauai is overrun with **chickens**. They're everywhere. The theory is that Hurricane Iniki knocked down all the chicken coops on the island, and the liberated chickens began happily reproducing in the absence of significant predators. Well, there are lots of **feral cats** on Kauai too, but the chickens seem to be winning.

They're kind of cute – until a rooster decides to start crowing outside your window at 4:30am. This is more likely to occur in a neighborhood home or a condo surrounded by natural foliage, but even fancy hotels are not immune. At least they will likely have air conditioning so you can close your windows.

When we lived in the Baby Beach neighborhood (near the Poipu round-about) in 2011, we would hear roosters in the distance, but they weren't close enough to wake us up. One morning we heard crowing, gradually getting louder and louder. Armen threw on his shorts and slippers and ran outside. Sure enough, a young rooster and his girlfriend were sauntering down the middle of the road toward our house, looking for a new place to settle down. Armen chased them all the way up the block until they got the idea. Thankfully they didn't return, at least during our time there.

Another noisy critter is the **cane toad**. A male cane toad will emit his mating call at periodic intervals throughout the night. The sound is a cross between a cow mooing and a squeaky gate hinge, and it's loud. The delay between his calls is approximately 10 seconds less than it takes for you to get back to sleep again. During one of our stays at Waikomo Stream Villas, a cane toad in the pond was advertising his services to the lady toads all night.

Tip: There's not much you can do. Close your windows. Use earplugs. Alcohol may help.

If you're lucky, you'll meet a **shama** – the full name is the white-rumped shama. Shamas are cage songbirds that were released in Kauai in the 1930s, and have thrived. It has a beautiful, complex multi-part song that seems unique to each individual bird. We've heard stories of people teaching them new song fragments to incorporate. We've seen shamas all over the island. They seem to favor shady areas with lots of trees and other foliage. They're curious about humans and not too shy – they will even follow us around. We have a short video of a shama singing on our Facebook page.

Albatrosses raise their chicks on Kauai. The nest is just a little spot on the ground where the parents leave the chick completely alone while they're out fishing – sometimes for days! With this somewhat neglectful parenting style it may not be a surprise that the albatross is endangered, so there are experts on Kauai that monitor the chicks and educate humans about keeping their dogs away from nesting areas. See Na 'Aina Kai Botanical Gardens for an albatross encounter that we had.

In areas with lots of shade and foliage but not much breeze, **mosquitoes** can be a problem. We've found that bug repellent with Picaridin works just as well as DEET, but without the strong odor and tendency to melt plastic and nylon. We're not going back to DEET. We prefer wipes because they pack easily in a carry-on and slip into your pocket, and they don't dose everyone around you like sprays do. Don't forget to lightly wipe your thin tee shirts and socks – mosquitos can punch right through those.

Driving on Kauai

You'll need a car to enjoy Kauai. It's not a big island, but the sights are all spread out. If you try to stay in the area around one hotel or resort, you'll miss just about everything.

The Ends of the Road

There are three distinct "end of the road" spots on Kauai, and they're each beautiful in their own way. Because Kauai's rugged terrain prevented a road from being all the way around the island (they tried and failed), these remote areas remain treasures for us to enjoy.

- To the north, past Hanalei, the road ends at Ke'e Beach (see Beaches) and the start of the Kalalau Trail (see Hikes and Walks). This is a tropical, exotic end of the road.
- To the west, past Kekaha, the road ends at Barking Sands and Polihale (see Beaches). This is a dry, remote end of the road.
- Up the Waimea Canyon, the road ends at the stunning Pu'u o Kila lookout (see Activities). It's chilly and windy up there, at around 4,000 feet of elevation – the high altitude end of the road.

Rental Options

If you don't want a shiny new car to instantly identify you as a tourist, consider saving some money and renting a car from Pete and Valerie at Kauai Rent a Car. Their cars are **not new**, but they work and they're cheap – sometimes less than half the cost. Our favorites are small SUVs like the Mazda Tribute or Hyundai Santa Fe – they have a little more ground clearance for bumpy roads.

They'll leave the car for you in the airport parking lot with the key under the mat, and they'll call you with directions for finding it when you land. Easy-peasy. Remember, these are old cars (some over 10 years old), but they're fine and you'll fit right in with the locals. If something breaks Pete will take care of it pronto. Remember all the money you're saving.

If you're a Costco member, check out their car rental page too. We recently rented a car from one of the major companies through the Costco web site, and we paid even less than Pete and Valerie's price. That won't happen every time, but it's worth a look.

> Tip: You might want to consider an SUV like a Jeep Cherokee. They are more expensive, but they really soak up the bumps on the roads to Maha'ulepu and Polihale (see Beaches), making the driving time a lot shorter and less stressful. Also, when you're driving on back roads, the higher seating position lets you see over the foliage for a better view.

Some have asked us whether a convertible is worth the extra expense. We've rented a convertible on Kauai twice. They have much less room, both in the back seat and the trunk. They **really** identify you as a tourist. The ground clearance is lower, making bumpy roads more difficult. A lot of the time you'll have the top up anyway, for protection from rain or excessive sun. But if there's just one or two of you, a convertible can be pretty sweet. Your call.

One Lane Bridges

Another way to instantly expose yourself as a tourist is to cross a one-lane bridge incorrectly. A whole group of cars crosses together. If you're following another car, just keep going! If you're at the front of the line waiting to cross, wait for all the oncoming cars to come over, then it's your turn.

Sometimes there's a long line of cars all crossing at once. The etiquette is that once 5 or so cars have gone across, somebody should stop and let the opposing cars come across. This is true especially if there's a gap more than a car length – don't rush to catch up to the last car just to get across!

> Tip: On the way to Ke'e Beach near Hanalei, there is a pair of one-lane bridges with a tiny island between them. Don't stop on the island – treat the whole thing as one bridge.

Traffic

Yes, unfortunately there can be traffic jams on Kauai. The two worst places for traffic are south of Lihue, near Rice Road and Costco, and through Kapa'a on the east shore. The seemingly endless road construction doesn't help either – everything on Kauai works on Island Time. It can be a bit frustrating, but hey, at least you're still on Kauai. Just roll down the windows, turn on a local radio station, and relax. We recommend KSRF "Da Pa'ina" at 95.9 FM for island and reggae music, and local ads with great Hawaiian accents. Or if you like traditional Hawaiian music, it's playing on 107.9 KTOH.

> Tip: If you need to get through Kapa'a and don't need to stop there for anything, try the Kapa'a bypass road. It's a bit longer, but it usually moves quickly. It runs through land that Bette Midler purchased to save it from being developed.

> Tip: There's a back road that avoids a lot of the traffic on Highway 50 south of Lihue. It's longer, but it winds

through countryside cane fields and forests, and is quite lovely. One end is Hulemalu Road at the Kauai Humane Society. The other end is at Nawiliwili Harbor in Lihue near Duke's Restaurant. There are side roads that branch off to the Wine Garden on Puhi Road, Costco and Kmart.

Merging with Aloha

If you see a two-lane stretch of highway in front of you, but everyone is lined up in just one lane – resist the impulse to race past everyone in the empty lane. The two lanes merge up ahead, and you'll just be exposing your lack of aloha spirit. As a local told us, "Nobody passes everyone else to cut in, because why are they more important than me?" Good point.

> Tip: One place this happens a lot is on Highway 50 heading south toward Poipu. Just before the left turn at the tree tunnel (Hwy 520), the two lanes merge into one. You won't see this in most mainland cities, but everyone on Highway 50 will wait patiently in the left lane with the right lane empty.

On a small island like Kauai, locals have learned that everyone knows each other, so they try to behave as though the other drivers are their friends and cousins. Many times they actually are!

Groceries and Supplies

Costco

Kauai has a great Costco in Lihue, about 10 minutes from the airport. It's a normal Costco with these improvements:

1. Hawaiians work there.
2. The free samples are huge. Probably because Hawaiians work there.
3. For some reason, no matter how busy it seems to be, it's pretty easy to find parking.
4. The prices aren't adjusted up to Hawaiian levels, so there are great bargains.
5. There's a large Hawaiian specialty section. This is the place to get Anahola Granola. There's also cold Hawaiian food like sesame seaweed salad and kalua pork in the deli case, and a five-pack of papaya in the fruit section.
6. If the seafood stand is open (usually Friday & Saturday), get some poke (the wasabi and the spicy are our favorites – they'll give you samples). If the stand isn't open, they often have the same poke in a cold case in the deli area at the back of the store.

Tip: Look for the six-pack of brown rice bowls in the Costco rice aisle. They microwave in 90 seconds and are so delicious with cold poke on top! Trust us on this.

7. The meat section has local seafood catches. Pick up some Ahi to grill. If you're lucky, they'll have some Monchong in – Lori's favorite fish. It's delicious grilled or broiled with a little olive oil and pepper. It will stick to the grill, so use extra oil or cook it on a piece of foil.

Tip: Here's a great Hawaiian breakfast. Scoop out half a papaya and squeeze some lime juice over it. Fill with plain Greek yogurt and your favorite berries. Sprinkle some Anahola Granola on top. Ono!

Other Stores

The new **Safeway** store in Lihue (near Costco) is modern and beautiful. They have a great selection of food and beverages, and there's a Starbucks inside. But here's the main reason to go: they are one of the rare Safeway stores with a **Chicken Wing Bar**. Most of the flavors are fine but pretty basic, except for one: the **salt and vinegar wings** are amazingly delicious and addictive. We stopped back a few times during our visit just to get more of them. If they're out of that flavor, ask the deli when the next batch will be ready. We've seen a crowd form while waiting for them.

There's a **Walmart** in Lihue near the airport, and a **Kmart** farther south in Lihue. They're both good places to get cheap souvenirs. The Walmart carries multiple varieties of Spam. Yes, there are multiple varieties of Spam. For some reason Spam is really big in Hawaii. Armen has been known to make fried Spam sandwiches – salty and delicious.

Speaking of souvenirs, you might want to do a quick stop at **Hilo Hattie** in Lihue, right near the airport. They have tons of Hawaiian clothes, hats, souvenirs, etc. It's very touristy but fun.

Want a nice Hawaiian shirt but don't want to spend the money? Try the **Salvation Army Thrift Store** on Rice Road in Lihue. As in any thrift shop there are great bargains, but here you can also find tropical clothing, boogie boards and other island gear. You can stop in when you have lunch at nearby Hamura Saimin or a beer at Kauai Beer Company (see Restaurants).

The **CVS** near Macy's in the Kukui Grove Shopping Center (Lihue on Nawiliwili Road, along the main highway) is a regular drugstore, but with tons of unique trinkets and interesting Asian snacks.

18

Need your **Starbucks**? The two we go to are:

- Kukui Grove Shopping Center (in Lihue, turn off the main highway onto Nawiliwili Road)
- Poipu Shopping Village in Poipu

There's also a Starbucks near the Safeway in Kapa'a.

Big Save Markets are all over Kauai. They aren't that cheap, but they have everything you'll need and they're charming. We usually go to the one in Koloa because it's near where we stay in Poipu. It's at the east end of the main road in Koloa.

For even more local and charming, check out the **Kukui'ula Market** by the yellow submarine at the round-about in Poipu. The place looks dubious, but they have basic groceries and local food.

While you're on Kauai you really need to try some poke ("POKE ay"). You might be able to get it at Costco, as noted above. Other places that have good poke are **Fish Express** in Lihue, and **Koloa Fish Market** in Koloa. The Koloa Fish Market is **cash only** – look for the paper sign that says "by order of management, no checks or credit cards – **9/95**." Oh Kauai, don't ever change.

The Wine Garden on Puhi Road in Lihue (right at the main highway) has a nice selection of beer, wine and some cigars too. That's where we've bought one of Armen's favorite beers – Piraat (Belgian).

Living Foods is a small trendy upscale grocery store in The Shops at Kukui'ula, also on the round-about in Poipu. They have nice produce, local products and a restaurant section. All pricey though.

New to The Shops at Kukui'ula is **Longs Drugs**, part of CVS. They have friendly folks working there and the prices are decent for Kauai. If you're overheated, they have very competent air conditioning.

Farmer's Markets are great on Kauai – there's a market somewhere every single day. At the airport you can pick up a guide to them. Our favorite is the Monday noon market at the ball field in Koloa. You need to rush in there with the crowd at noon to get the best stuff. Watch out or a local grandma might knock you down.

There's also a **Wednesday outdoor market** at The Shops at Kukui'ula at the Poipu round-about. Vendors sell produce and all kinds of food there. One of Armen's favorites is pie from Right Slice – their chocolate coconut macadamia is amazing. Lori always helps with it too. If you miss getting pie here, you can also get it at Hanapepe Art Night (see Activities). Another treat is to taste the jams and preserves (both sweet and savory)  at Monkeypod Jam – say hi to Aletha from us! She also has a store with coffee and pastries in Lawai, right on Highway 50.

Hikes and Walks

Kauai's true beauty opens up even more when you park your car and start walking. There are dozens of hikes on the island - here are a few that you can try.

You'll need to wear good walking shoes that can get muddy, and a hat is a good idea. Make sure you pack enough water – you'll need more than you think if it's hot. We always take some food along so that we can have a bite to eat at an amazing viewpoint.

Telescoping hiking poles can be really handy on Kauai trails. They can secure your footing on slippery or crumbling rocks, provide stability climbing up and down steep sections, and provide a pivot point when hopping over a stream. Some people use two of them, but we find that one works great. Set the length of the pole so that your forearm is level when your elbow is at your side. They may fit into your luggage easier if you separate the sections.

If you're hiking in shady jungle areas, juice up with bug repellent before you go. See **Kauai Wildlife**.

> Tip: Whenever you're hiking on Kauai, make sure you're stepping on solid trail. Sometimes there will be vegetation right next to the trail, and you'd think there is rock underneath it. Sometimes it's just air. We've heard that people have been killed by stepping off the trail this way.

> Tip: Take flash flood warnings seriously. A creek can go from a trickle to a flood in just minutes. While we were on Kauai recently, someone drowned while trying to cross a rising creek – and that was on a *guided hike*. Alerts are sent out by cell phone, but you need to use your judgment too.

Waimea Canyon

Po'omau Canyon/Ditch Trail

The UKG has a good description of this trail, but we don't think it does it  full justice. The trailhead is near the Kokee Lodge up the Waimea Canyon road – follow the exact directions in the UKG. The hike to the finger ridge isn't difficult – maybe an hour each way depending on how close to the trailhead you can park. There are some up and down sections with brief glimpses of the canyon, and small creek crossings, but no continuous long climbs. After about 45 minutes on the trail, watch for the trail branching off to the left – that's where the big pay-off is. The view out on the finger ridge is stunning – we both cried. Try to imagine a wrap-around view from a perch out in the middle of the Waimea Canyon, with mountains, forests, waterfalls, goats – got it? Sorry, you're not even close. You need to see it for yourself.

> Tip: The UKG describes the entire hike, but the first section to the finger ridge and back is probably the most bang for your buck.

> Tip: Take some lunch and eat it at the End of Trail sign out on the ridge.

Canyon Trail to WaiPo'o Falls

This is a moderately strenuous hike that takes about an hour each way, if you can park at the trailhead. If you have to walk down the road, add maybe 30 more minutes each way. If the road looks dry, a  basic two-wheel-drive SUV shouldn't have any trouble, but you should think carefully before taking a low-clearance rental car down there. AAA probably won't come to rescue you here.

The nice thing about this hike is the views along the trail – they're amazing. The payoff at the end of the hike is the pair of waterfalls. To the left is a small falls and a pool (look for the narrow trail that skirts a big boulder). We didn't swim in it, but you can if you want, especially if the day is really warm. To the right is a stunning view from the top of a huge waterfall pouring into the abyss of the Waimea Canyon. Don't get too close to the edge – it's a long way down.

We are split on whether we like this hike better than the Ditch Trail. Armen likes the Ditch Trail better, because the payoff at the end is so stunning, and it's nice and quiet. Lori likes the Canyon Trail for its better views along the way, and the cool waterfalls, but they make a huge racket, as do the helicopters constantly buzzing in for a look.

Tip: Hike them both!

Grand Loop Trail

We're proud to say we did this one. It will take most of the day. It's about 11 miles – down,

across, and back up. See how that works, the "back up" is at the end of the hike? It just about killed us – a long, continuous uphill slog for about 2.5 miles and 2,000 feet elevation back to the car. However, if you're in good hiking condition and want to see some unbelievable sights, go for it! UKG has good directions on this one. We got up there fairly early (by 9am), left our car at the upper (farther on the road) trailhead, and then hitchhiked down to the lower trailhead by the Kokee Lodge. We wouldn't hitchhike anywhere else, but it was fine there. In fact, the very first car stopped for us. It was totally worth it to not have to hike the mile or two along the road to the lower trailhead.

It was on this trail that a wild boar ran across the trail right in front of Lori. Her first thought was "I wonder whom that big black dog belongs to?" Her next thought was "whoa, that's a wild boar!" Fortunately it was just passing through – apparently they can be vicious. We've never seen another one, but you can see the torn-up dirt from them digging all along the hiking trails.

> Tip: If you don't want to do the whole loop, you can just go down and back on the Nu'alolo Trail (the lower trailhead) or the Awa'awapuhi Trail (the upper trailhead). They connect down at the bottom to make the loop. Doing just one or the other will reduce your

hike by a couple of miles, but honestly, doing the whole loop is worth it to see more sights without retracing your steps.

Note: The cross trail connecting the two to make a loop is officially closed due to a slide near the Nu'alolo end as of July 2016, but we've heard that you can still cross the slide area if you're careful, and at your own risk.

South Shore

Maha'ulepu Beach Walk

See Beaches for directions to Maha'ulepu. From the farthest parking area at Kawailoa Bay, take the trail to the left as you face the ocean. Along the trail there are stunning views of the rocks and crashing  waves, and sometimes windsurfers out in the bay. There's a dry blowhole that sounds like a dragon is sleeping under the trail. If you keep going, there are amazing weathered rock promontories, crashing waves, open meadows, hidden beaches, and a peaceful stone labyrinth that was built as a tribute to a family member. If you feel adventurous you can cross the fence line and find another cove and beach.

Shipwreck Beach Walk

This is a gorgeous oceanfront walk that's not too hard. You can vary the distance just by turning around and going back whenever you feel like it. Drive past the Hyatt in  Poipu, and turn right on Ainako to get down to the beach parking lot. (The sign for Ainako road wasn't visible the last time we visited – just turn between the Hyatt and the golf course.) If the lot is full, just wait a minute, someone will be leaving soon, or park on the side of the road. Facing the ocean, walk to the left (either on the trail through the trees, or on the beach) and go up to the rocky lookout – it's a stunning view.

People (not us!) sometimes jump from there to the water 37 feet below. After the jump, it's a long swim back to the beach.

 We once saw a huge manta ray feeding along here. It was hard to tell its size, but judging from swimmers in the water, it was probably at least 10 feet across.

From the lookout, continue on the trails to the left. If you keep going, you'll see eroded rock formations, little sandy beaches, a golf course, and eventually you'll end up at Makauwahi Cave and Maha'ulepu Beach. But we recommend you drive to those instead (see Sights and Beaches).

East Shore

Nounou Mountain Trail (aka Sleeping Giant)

From anywhere on the east side, like in Wailua, you can see a mountain that some say looks like a giant man sleeping on his back. Maybe smoking some pakalolo (marijuana)  helps. Regardless, you can climb to the summit, which is about 3.5 miles each way. The whole thing might take 4 hours or so, including breaks and enjoying the views.

There are three trails that meet before the final ascent, all mentioned in the UKG. We decided to take the one from Kuamoo road (Hwy 580), a few miles mauka (inland) from Wailua. We just parked by the road.

The beginning of the trail is not very strenuous, and it has a lot of tree cover. It can get a bit buggy through there – juice up if it's a problem. After the trails converge, it gets steeper. The picnic table area has some great views, but if it's dry and you're feeling confident, you can go farther (ahead and to the left) on the trail that leads to the summit. You'll go past the End of Trail sign with its dire warnings. The UKG makes it sound like you're one false step away from death, but we didn't find it to be that bad. Use your own judgment. The summit has more amazing views. We didn't go down to the giant's "chin" from the summit, but some people do.

East Kauai Path

This a smooth, paved path that heads north along the ocean from Kapaa. It's a leisurely stroll more than a hike – great for all ages and abilities. You can park in Kapaa and head north, or you can start midway from Kealia Beach just north of Kapaa. The ocean views are beautiful along here. If you want to bike it instead, see **Coconut Coasters** in Activities.

North Shore

Kalalau Trail

This hike begins from Ke'e Beach (see Beaches). Don't let the description intimidate you – they list the first stop at 2 miles for Hanakapi'ai Beach (which we have hiked to), but there are amazing views within the first 15 minutes of the hike. You can check them out and go back down if you like. The trail can be a bit steep and rugged, so you might not want to wear your slippers (Hawaiian for flip flops).

Food and Drink

South Shore

Puka Dog

At least once you should cave in and have a Puka Dog, in Poipu Shopping Village. It's near Poipu Beach, so you can stop in if you're starving and you need something quick. Puka means "hole" in Hawaiian. They poke a hole in a soft hotdog bun (instead of slicing it), toast it from the inside, inject sauce into it and push the hotdog in there. Make sure you add the lilikoi mustard. A guilty pleasure – you know you want to try it. We won't tell anyone. They also serve real fresh-squeezed lemonade.

Keoki's Paradise

This is a cheesy quintessential Hawaiian place in the Poipu Shopping Village, complete with tiki torches lit at dusk and mediocre live Hawaiian music. But sometimes that's exactly what you need. The food is okay, the service is friendly, and the prices are not too unreasonable. There are two sections of the restaurant. Eat in the more casual section for lower prices.

> Tip: You might want to juice up – it's garden dining, so there are some mosquitos.

> Tip: The Hula Pie is awesome if you saved some room.

The Beach House

Everyone talks about The Beach House (along Lawai Rd on the way to Spouting Horn), but we've never actually eaten there. Sure, the sunsets are amazing, but you can sit right in front of the restaurant and watch those for free. (Recently they roped off part of their lawn area, but there's still plenty of room.) And we've heard the food is just okay for the high prices. Try it if you want and let us know on our Facebook page – maybe it's awesome.

Kalaheo Café and Coffee Company

This is a great place to have breakfast or lunch. They serve dinner too, but we haven't tried that. It's right along the highway in Kalaheo, so there's no view, but the people are nice and the food is good.

East Shore

Hamura Saimin
This rough-looking little place in Lihue is the place to go for saimin noodles (similar to ramen or pho). You just go in and wait for a spot to open up. You'll probably strike up conversations with locals or other visitors – it's a great experience.

> Tip: Cash only!

Kauai Beer Company
This is a fun place right on Rice Road, near the Salvation Army and Hamura Saimin. Being from Seattle, we admit to being a bit snobby about beer. The beer here is good, maybe not great, and the service is friendly. You can sit inside or outside, and you can build your own flights of 4 ounce pours. Lori loved the Kauai Juice Company kombucha they have on tap. We were just expecting basic pub food, but we were surprised by how fresh and delicious the bruschetta was, and the pork sandwich is also ono. There are often food trucks nearby for other dining options.

> Tip: If you happen to be in Kauai on the first Friday in December, there's a great parade called Lights on Rice (we smile every time we say it). Kauai Beer Company is a great place to watch it. Get there at least an hour early – it's very popular with the locals!

Duke's
Duke's is on the beach in front of the Marriott near the airport in Lihue. If you drive along Rice Rd, you can find parking in a little lot next to the hill and take a footbridge over to the restaurant. We've eaten at both the fancy upstairs section, and

the more casual downstairs. Downstairs is cheaper of course, and that's what we recommend if you want to go. It's a lovely atmosphere right on the sand, but the food really isn't that great for the price. Maybe you should stop by for one last drink or snack before you go to the airport.

Mermaids

Mermaids is a taco window in Kapa'a, right on the main road. The food is pretty good and the people-watching is fun. It's amazing to see the activity in that tiny kitchen. There's limited outdoor seating on the sidewalk.

Tiki Tacos

This place is in Kapa'a, just off the main road on the mauka (inland) side in a little strip mall. It looks a little rough - you might not venture in there if you didn't know how good the tacos are. The corn tortillas are handmade, and the fish is fantastic. We like the Mayan taco the best – it has a wonderful roasted flavor.

> Tip: We heard the owner say "positive" as an affirmation, instead of "okay" or "cool". We think it should catch on everywhere – we could all use more positive, right?

Hukilau Lanai

Hukilau means fishing using nets, and also a beach party. Lanai is of course the word for patio or deck. Hukilau Lanai is a restaurant in Kapa'a that's inside the Kauai Coast Resort. The service, garden view and food are very good.

> Tip: Call for reservations for the Tasting Menu. It's only $32 for five small courses, or $50 if you want to add a wine tasting for each course. That's reasonable for

Kauai. They have specific seating times for the Tasting Menu, usually early (starting at 5pm). You want to be early anyway, because the evening light in the garden is lovely before sunset.

North Shore

Hanalei Dolphin

Just before you get to Hanalei town, the Dolphin is on your right. They have good fish tacos, cold beer and friendly service.

> Tip: Sit at an outside table and watch the stand-up paddleboarders going by on the river.

Kauai Ono

Kauai Ono is a tent/food truck dining experience in Princeville that focuses on local gourmet ingredients. It only runs certain  nights and you need a reservation. We are a bit mixed on this one. It's a really unique and cool experience, and because you sit at communal tables, you'll meet other people and talk story, which is fun. The food is very high quality, locally sourced and expertly prepared. However, it isn't cheap - $60 per person, and you need to bring your own wine (they have an ice bucket to keep it cold). The dinner lasts two hours, which seems like a long time for 5 courses, but weirdly felt slightly rushed. If you're a foodie and want a different dining experience, you should do it. We're glad we tried it, but once is probably enough for us.

Tip: Your credit card holds the reservation, but you actually pay separately after the meal. They *really* prefer you pay with cash – who wouldn't? – but if you must you can use your credit card.

Tip: You should juice up on bug repellent. You'll want to do it at your car – the wait staff will ask you to step away from the dining area to avoid chemical smells near the food. Bug wipes with Picaridin instead of DEET are a good choice, because they don't have a strong odor.

Tip: If you want a good 5-course meal for less money even including wine, see **Hukilau Lanai** on the east shore.

Tiki Iniki

A fun, cool tiki bar with kitschy tropical décor, wild colors and interesting drinks served in tiki god glasses. We didn't try the food, but we've seen mixed reviews – maybe you should stick with drinking. Todd Rundgren's  wife Michele is the owner, and the servers are fun and boisterous. Tiki Iniki is tucked into Princeville Center at the "food court" – look for the signs, since you won't see the establishment itself from the parking lot.

Activities

South Shore

Makauwahi Cave
This is a fascinating place that is an active archeological site (follow the directions for Maha'ulepu Beaches in Beaches). It's a collapsed open air cave, but to get inside you do need to crouch down and walk through a short rock tunnel. If the cave is open for visitors, the field to your right (just past the light blue shack) will not have a chain across the entrance. Guided tours are Wed, Fri, Sat and Sun from 10-2. It's Kauai though, so don't get too attached to schedules. If it's closed, at least you're almost to Maha'ulepu.

Spouting Horn
This is a natural blowhole that shoots water up into the air with the wave action. It's a mile or two from the round-about in Poipu. It's worth a look if you're in the area anyway. There are also merchant stalls selling stuff, and lots of chicken families (birds, not humans) wandering around.

> Tip: You can see a nice view of Spouting Horn in the distance if you drive past it to the end of the road and turn around at the gate. Pull over to the side and take in the scene. Native vegetation has been re-introduced and encouraged here. In the spring whales have their calves along this coast.

Turtles in Whaler's Cove

We haven't seen this in other guide books. Find Whaler's Cove condos on Puuholo Rd. just south of the round-about in Poipu. At the left end of their parking lot are stairs leading down to the cove. Disregard the No Trespassing signs. The cove is public access; those signs are for the weak-minded. Park on the street if you're concerned. In the evening during fall and winter months, sea turtles come in to rest in this little cove. We have seen dozens of them in there (that was in the fall, and we've seen them in November and December too). The best time to go is about 30 minutes before sunset. If the surf and wind are very quiet, you can heard them inhale when they come up to breathe. Magical.

Kauai Coffee

You can take a self-guided tour of the coffee plantation, learn how coffee is grown and processed, and taste many varieties of their coffee. They also have one of our favorite gift shops, with the common stuff and also some unique things too.

Allerton Garden

Whether you're into plants or not, this place is amazing. It's part of the National Tropical Botanical Garden near the end of Lawai Road from the Poipu round-about, right across from Spouting Horn. They have guided walking tours that are not too strenuous. There are plants, flowers, trees, fruit, statuary, etc. The guides are all very knowledgeable and friendly – Sam is especially good. Load up on bug juice in the waiting area before you get on the bus.

> Tip: There's an adjacent garden called McBride with a self-guided tour. It's okay too, but we like Allerton better.

For a special evening, we recommend the Allerton Sunset Tour. It may not be offered every day – make a reservation. You get to see areas of the garden that aren't on the regular tours, including the Allerton house and beach area. The tour includes dinner, which at this writing in July 2016 is catered by Living Foods in Poipu. (We've heard the new menu is okay, but the food isn't the main draw anyway.) The Robert Allerton story is very interesting – he was a wealthy man who loved art and nature, and he designed and built the whole estate. He wanted to leave his estate to the man he loved and lived with, but the laws wouldn't allow that. So Robert adopted him as his "son". The authorities closed that loophole immediately afterward.

Tip: The Allerton tours are a bit pricey. If it makes you feel better, your money supports their noble efforts, and it may be tax deductible (ask your bean counter). If you book online at least a day in advance they often have discount codes.

Hanapepe Art Night

The tiny town of Hanapepe has an "art night" every Friday evening from 6-9. All the stores stay open late (well, 9pm is late by Kauai standards) and there are street vendors and music. The "art" is in several of the stores, which sell work by local artists. A cool bookstore is there too (see **Talk Story** in Activities). We enjoy Art Night, and we purchased a small etching at one of the shops, but it's pretty low-key and might not be for everyone.

Tip: Find the pedestrian bridge over the river (there's a path between two buildings, on the same side as Talk Story Bookstore). Standing out there at night is pretty cool.

Talk Story Bookstore

If you're into books, or even if you're not, Talk Story in Hanapepe is worth a visit. Their claim is that they're the westernmost independent bookstore in the United States – hopefully nobody will  open one in Kekaha. You can go to Talk Story anytime, but you can also combine it with your visit to **Hanapepe Art Night**.

The owner, Ed Justus, will likely greet you when you enter, and offer to take you on a tour of the store. Say yes! You'll likely discover something new in their charmingly curated and eclectic collection.

> Tip: The phrase "talk story" is Hawaiian slang for "shoot the breeze" or chit chat. It does not mean gossip or talking bad about people – that's "talk stink". You don't want to talk stink on Kauai – it's a very small island. Actually that's a pretty good rule everywhere.

Kauai Kookie Factory

Kauai Kookies can be found in stores all over the island, but if you go to the source in Hanapepe you can find lots of flavors and styles that aren't sold anywhere else. If you like your sweets, it's worth stopping in if you're heading through Hanapepe anyway.

> Tip: Even though it really is the factory where they're made, there are no tours of the production facility – just the shop.

Hyatt Hotel

We like walking through the lobby and down to the beach. There are all kinds of swimming pools (salt and fresh water), trails and benches to explore. Take a picnic! Nobody will know you aren't staying there if you're cool about it. You can also support them by buying a $15 mai tai at the bar.

> Tip: You can also park at Shipwreck Beach (see Beaches) and just walk around the fence into the Hyatt pool area.

Tip: There's a waterslide, but you need a hotel wristband to use it.

Kauai Humane Society – Dog Field Trip

The Kauai Humane Society has a modern facility on Hwy 50 just west of Lihue. To help their dogs socialize and get adopted, they'll let you check one out for a field trip. They'll give you a towel, leash, treats and an awesome "Adopt Me" vest (for the dog, not you). You can take the dog on an adventure for an hour or a whole day. We took "Little Boy" out for a few hours on a recent visit and we all had a lot of  fun. Having a dog is a great conversation starter when meeting both locals and other visitors.

West Shore

Waimea Hawaiian Church

This isn't for everyone, but do you want to hear some serious spiritual hymn singing? Go to the Hawaiian church. Their service is Sunday at 9am. You'll probably be the only mainlanders in there. The whole thing is in Hawaiian, so you won't understand a word, though the last time we visited the pastor's wife sat next to us in the back row and showed us in the hymnal which songs they were singing. When they stand and sing in harmony, it's time for chicken skin (Hawaiian slang for goose bumps). We've asked members of the congregation how they learned to sing that way, and they said they just pick it up from when they're keiki (children). The whole service lasts about an hour to 90 minutes. Throw some bucks in the offering basket – it's aloha spirit. The church is on the ocean side of the main road, a white building in Waimea.

> Tip: For some reason they're in stealth mode on most navigation systems – if you find Wrangler's Steakhouse or Big Save in Waimea, you're there.

Waimea Canyon

Sometime during your visit you really must drive up the Waimea Canyon and check out the viewpoints. If you can get to the last viewpoint (Pu'u o Kila) in the morning (see the UKG), you'll have a better chance of a fantastic view (that's our front cover photo). There are many times later in the day when you're just staring into a cloud bank, wondering what all the fuss is about.

> Tip: The UKG says to drive up from Waimea on 550, then drive back down on Koke'e road (552) to Kekaha. We don't agree. It's better to drive **up** by following the main signs through Kekaha. Then, when you're coming back **down**, take a left onto 550 and treat yourself to amazing views on the way down into Waimea.

East Shore

Luau at Smith's Tropical Paradise

We're calling this an activity because luaus are more about the experience than the food. The only luau we've done (several times) is at Smith's Tropical Paradise in Wailua.

It's set in a beautiful garden area, and there's even a little tram you can ride around for a narrated tour of the flora and fauna (including peacocks). The food is basic good luau food, and the mai tais are plentiful. They'll help to fully enjoy the cheesy, but often beautiful dancing show after dinner. Make a reservation.

> Tip: Poi is only horrible if you try to eat it by itself. Dip some kalua pork into it. Ono!

Kauai Hindu Monastery

This barely gets a mention in UKG, but we love it. Craftsmen are working on a Hindu Temple – carving it by hand from granite. They've been at it for

decades, and it's not done yet. You can see the beautiful outer grounds any time, but to go on the free tour and see the stone temple itself, you need to make a reservation (because parking is so limited) by calling 888-735-1619. You'll learn a bit about Hinduism and their project. You need to dress modestly – there are shawls for you to borrow if needed.

> Tip: Load up on insect repellent before you go in. Those Hindu mosquitos are particularly aggressive for some reason. Someone asked our tour guide whether it was okay to slap a mosquito, given the Hindu principles of non-violence. He said that he considered it "home invasion" so it was okay.

Coconut Coasters - Bike Rentals

The UKG barely mentions bike rentals, and we were lukewarm on the idea at first, but we were surprised at how much we loved renting a couple of old-school beach coasters and

riding up and down the paved trail along the ocean. The Coconut Coasters shop is at the north end of Kapaa on the ocean side. The bikes were super smooth and easy to pedal, the path has only gentle inclines, and the ocean views when you ride to the north are gorgeous. You can even get a basket to carry your stuff. An hour is minimum, but you should get 2 hours if you want to explore both directions with time for stops. The trail was very quiet on the day we did it – John the shopkeeper said that it's usually busier. You might want to choose a morning or afternoon time, since there isn't a lot of shade along the trail.

> Tip: If you're wearing any Seattle Seahawks gear, or maybe even if you say "Go Hawks!" to the shopkeeper, you can get a discount.

Kayaking

We did a kayak tour and hike to Secret Falls with Wailua Kayak Adventures, but there are a few companies that do this combination. You kayak up the (very gentle) Wailua River to the trailhead, then hike in to Secret Falls for lunch. Really fun.

> Tip: They tell you that rocks could possibly fall on your head if you stand under the falls. It's so fun, we did it for a minute anyway. We figure if your number's up, your number's up.

Tubing in Irrigation Tunnels

Kauai Backcountry Adventures in Lihue will take you up into the interior of Kauai to go tubing through old irrigation canals and tunnels. The UKG doesn't think it's that fun, but we really enjoyed it. The young guides are fun and energetic, and they'll tell you facts and tips about Kauai on the van rides and out on the trail and canals. The water can get moving pretty fast through the tunnels, so you spin and bounce off the walls for a fun ride. Lori bruised her knee on the tunnel wall, but she's pretty tough. The cost is a bit steep, but it's a unique adventure that we would do again with friends.

> Tip: The guides said we probably didn't need bug repellent since the water is moving pretty fast – but they didn't mention standing in the shade for the safety briefing! We got several bites. You should apply some

bug juice, especially on your ankles, when the van stops at the valley lookout or before walking down the trail to the launch point.

North Shore

Ziplining
At first we didn't know how fun this would be, but we did it with friends and it was a hoot. We went to Princeville Ranch Adventures. They have several choices available – we chose the one that ends with lunch at a swimming hole. Their front yard is where they pitch the tent for Kauai Ono (see Dining).

Na 'Aina Kai Botanical Gardens
If you go to just one botanical garden, go to Allerton Garden on the south shore. But this one is cool too, and the location is handy if you're staying up north. There's a guided tram tour that includes stops along the way to get off and walk a bit. The sculptures are great, and the explanations of native and invasive plant species are interesting. The highlight for us was seeing an albatross chick waiting for its parents to return from a fishing trip - in Alaska! Albatross expert Hob Osterlund happened to be there to check on the chick, and she gave us an impromptu lecture. See Kauai Wildlife for more about albatrosses.

Beaches
First, gear up for snorkeling and lounging. You can rent snorkel gear for the whole week – just leave it in the trunk of your car so it's always ready. You can rent gear just about anywhere, but Snorkel Bob's and Seasport Divers are safe bets. If you're staying in a condo, see if they already have beach chairs (check the closet). If not, rent them and leave them in the car! They

have the backpack-style Tommy Bahama chairs at the Seasport Divers at the Poipu round-about. Believe us – you'll be happy you have chairs for your beach time.

> Tip: Don't try to walk in fins; you might fall down, and you'll definitely look like a tourist. To get in the water, put your mask on first, then wade out in a sandy area until you're about waist-deep, holding your fins. Breathing through your snorkel, crouch down into the water between waves and put on your fins. When you're ready to get back onto land, reverse the process. Swim until the water is shallow, then crouch to remove your fins before walking out.

> Tip: When you're at the beach or on the rocks, keep one eye on the water. A big wave can sneak up and knock you down. When you walk out into the water, turn and stand sideways to the wave, legs apart, when a wave approaches. You'll have a better chance of staying upright.

You might encounter a monk seal resting at just about any beach on Kauai. We've seen them at Beach House/Lawai Road,

Poipu and Salt Ponds. They're endangered, and it's illegal to mess with them in any way. There's a volunteer monk seal response team (we're not kidding) that will put a rope barrier around a monk seal to remind dumb tourists to keep their distance.

Tip: Don't walk on the sand or in the shallow water between the seal and the water – they need a clear route to safety.

Kauai has **so many beaches**, and UKG has great descriptions. Here are a few of our favorites, along with what they're good for.

South Shore

Maha'ulepu Beaches (lounging, walking, secluded)

There are technically a few different beaches along this stretch, but we just call the whole thing Maha'ulepu. Let's cover the pronunciation – "mah HA leh poo"

Armen Stein Photography

(we don't really hear the first "u" pronounced). The specific beach we love, and visit every time, is **Kawailoa Bay**. It's great for lounging, reading, walking and shallow wading, but don't swim too far out – there's no protective reef. The trees are close to the water here, so they make some lovely shade. There are seldom many tourists at Kawailoa Bay – you might have a section of the beach all to yourself, especially on weekdays. And there's a great walk that starts from the last beach, Kawailoa Bay – see Hikes and Walks.

The road to Maha'ulepu is a bumpy one, but your rental car will be fine if you drive slowly and navigate around the deepest potholes. Go past the Hyatt in Poipu until the road turns to gravel. Go past CJM Stables and take a few turns (the alternatives will be gated closed). Eventually you'll reach a parking area with a muddy hole in the middle. This is Gillin's Beach. But **don't stop there** - keep driving down the dirt road to the left until you reach the end of the road at Kauailoa Bay, where there are more places to park. Drive out before 6pm — they lock the gates at dusk.

On the bumpy road to Maha'ulepu you'll go right past the guard shack marking the field leading to Makauwahi Cave (see Activities).

> Tip: If there's a tall rock, drive around it entirely, or at least drive over it with your tire rather than letting it pass down the middle of your car where it might hit something important.

Beach House/Lawai Road (snorkeling, lounging, sunset)

Lawai Road Beach is along the road to Spouting Horn, just a few minutes from the Poipu round-about. It is a small sandy beach right in front of the Beach House restaurant. The snorkeling there is usually very good, especially in the winter, and in the morning when the ocean is calmer. It's technically not "Lawai Beach", because that's actually another beach in Allerton Garden (see Activities), but some people call it that anyway.

Koloa Landing (snorkeling)

This isn't a beach, it's a rocky cove (Whaler's Cove) with a boat ramp that is popular with divers. You can find it on Hoonani Road just south of the Poipu round-about. The visibility is variable – it depends on the amount of run-off from the adjacent Waikomo Stream, and the swell coming in from the south. If you want to check it out before getting in, walk along the rock wall above the cove and look down into the water. If you can see the rocky bottom (polarized sunglasses are helpful) then the water is pretty clear. When conditions are right there are lots of fish and sea turtles to see.

Baby Beach (lounging, sunset)

This is a little local beach near the Poipu round-about. It's not good for much except for hanging out, reading, and watching the sunset with a beverage.

Wait, those are some of our favorite activities! Take Hoona Road off of Lawai Road, and find the path between two houses to reach the beach. Beaches are public land on Kauai, and there are little access trails hidden everywhere. They might not have signs, but it's totally fine to use them. During the week you'll often see local keiki (children) playing in the shallow lagoon. And the sunsets here are great, especially in the winter when

the sun is still setting into the water (in April it reaches the land). You'll often meet other people from the neighborhood (visitors and locals) who gather just to have a drink and watch the show. This is the only place we've ever seen the green flash.

Sheraton Beach (swimming, lounging, boogie boarding)

The Sheraton in Poipu has beautiful grounds right along the beach. You can take your chairs and sit at the beach, or find a little grassy area for yourself under the palm trees – heavenly. There are public parking lots on both ends of the complex, on the ocean side of the road.

Poipu Beach (lounging, sunset, swimming, snorkeling)

Poipu Beach is the quintessential Kauai beach. It has a protected shallow lagoon for swimming, a great snorkeling area, and lots of sandy beach for lounging and people-

watching. Yes, it's a popular beach, but we've always been able to find parking and our little spot of sand. Poipu Beach's distinguishing feature is the **tombolo**, an area of sand leading out to a rocky area. The waves wash up onto the shore from **both directions**, so at high tide you can stand in the middle and have water gently lapping at your feet from both sides.

Tombolos are very rare – apparently there are only three in all the Hawaiian Islands, they're all on Kauai, and Poipu is the only accessible one.

Brenneke's Beach (boogie boarding, lounging)

Over to the left across the grassy area (facing the water) from Poipu Beach is Brenneke's Beach. A lot of people enjoy boogie boarding here. Boogie boarding is easy to try – you can rent the gear (board & short flippers) right  across the street at Nukumoi or any of the other shops around. Just make sure there are lots of other people in the water, ideally some locals. If you're the only person out there, there's a reason – the conditions might be dangerous. At Brenneke's, make sure you don't ride all the way in, especially where the rocks are. Armen cut open his knee pretty good there one time.

> Tip: As the wave approaches, kick your fins to get started in the same direction. As the wave reaches you, push the front of the board down with your arms, so you start to slide down the "hill" of the wave.

Shipwreck Beach (lounging, boogie boarding)

This is a nice beach right next to the Hyatt Hotel. There's a rocky point on the left where crazy people jump into the water. See Hikes and Walks for directions.

Salt Ponds Park (swimming, lounging)

This is a pretty park with a nice sandy beach. The water is protected for swimming, but it's usually not clear enough for good snorkeling.

West Shore

Polihale Beach (vast, secluded, sunset, crashing waves)

Some people think that Polihale means "house of the afterlife", but it isn't creepy – it's just where people's spirits move on. The beach stretches for miles, and hardly anyone is there. A local once  advised us that "if Polihale gets too crowded, just walk a mile farther down." This is a great place to lounge, watch the surf crash onto the sand, and enjoy a picnic dinner or beverage while the sun sets. It is not a good place to be in the water, except for shallow wading in the surf. Keep one eye on the waves.

Getting there is an investment. You need to drive to the far west end of the island along the south shore, and then take about 5 miles of very bumpy, potholed road to get to the beaches. UKG has good directions. There are all kinds of warning signs, but if the road looks okay (i.e. dry enough), go for it – slowly and carefully. Rental car companies frown on driving to Polihale, but if you're feeling rebellious, it's a great adventure.

The first photo in this guide is of us at Polihale at sunset.

> Tip: If it seems to be raining everywhere else on Kauai, drive west. Polihale and the other western parts of Kauai are the driest areas on the island.

North Shore

Ke'e Beach (lounging, sunset, snorkeling, hiking)

Pronounced "Kay AY". This is one of most stunning sunset spots on Kauai, but it's a drive to get there, especially from the south shore. Go past Hanalei to the end of the road – literally. Snorkeling here is really good when the conditions are right, especially in the summer, because there's a protective reef. The Kalalau Trail along the Na Pali coast also starts here – see Hikes and Walks.

Hideaways (lounging, seclusion, swimming)

If you're up for a steep (but not too long) trail, Hideaways is a great beach that many tourists won't attempt. It's in the Princeville area – UKG has good  directions. Armen once snorkeled with a sea turtle here – so cool. Watch the conditions before going in the water – winters can be rough.

Larsen's Beach (lounging, being naked)

Remote and unofficially clothing-optional. Otherwise a pretty boring beach without reef protection.

Made in the USA
San Bernardino, CA
10 April 2017